House with a Dark Sky Roof

T. ZACHARY COTLER'S poems have appeared in *Paris Review, Poetry, The Wolf*, and other journals in the US and UK. In 2006, he was awarded the Amy Clampitt Fellowship by the late poet's estate. He is a founding editor of *The Winter Anthology*. This is his first book of poems.

House with a Dark Sky Roof

T. Zachary Cotler

SALT

London

PUBLISHED BY SALT PUBLISHING
Dutch House, 307–308 High Holborn, London WC1V 7LL United Kingdom

© T. Zachary Cotler, 2011

The right of T. Zachary Cotler to be identified as the
author of this work has been asserted by him in accordance
with Section 77 of the Copyright, Designs and Patents Act 1988.

Salt Publishing 2011

Printed and bound in the United States by Lightning Source Inc

Typeset in Swift 9.5 / 13

ISBN 978 1 84471 820 7 paperback

1 3 5 7 9 8 6 4 2

Contents

Acknowledgements

Some of these poems first appeared in the following publications:

32 Poems, American Poetry Journal, Antioch Review, Barrow Street, Crab Orchard Review, Denver Quarterly, FIELD, The Journal, Paris Review, Poetry, Poetry Daily, Poetry Salzburg Review, Portland Review, Post Road, Puerto Del Sol, Republic of Letters, Southern Review, Stickman Review, Subtropics, Third Coast, Verse Daily, and *West Branch.*

First Thaw

At the rim of a sloped field of goldenrod, pressed
all winter by snow downhill so the whole
dead field resembles the side of a thatched hut, terrain
that was impassable on foot
in summer,   he observes two contrails
crossed, with a half-day-moon   in the deep
                              pocket of the crux,
the crux feathering, diffusing
into thought-parts,
white stabs,
X
X
X in a line,
              not a timeline exactly,
but a rhythmic series
of "batteries" (a
line of full "bowls"
of visual thought)
                    laid out, as if ready to discharge precipitous
mental change, so he shepherds his view
down the slope and further field devoid
of evidence of humans
other than a leather jacket,
thrown over a yard-high, sapling pine. There is a
peripheral   red blip/streak:

too quickly, the shepherd
thinks down the slope
to say what it was: streak of mutant
                    autumn mid-spring?
                    Mere siren,
police or fire, in the town
behind the hills: Doppler stars: red open
valves deoxidizing blue,
whole royal families of porphyriacs,

collapsed around their harpsichords inlaid with cameos
of jasperware and purpleheart,
dying of nosebleeds:
                    hemorrhaging data
from embassies in twenty countries accruing on GhostNet in China,
exposed today, March 29th, 2009. Foreign ministry spokesman Qin Gang:
                    "China is opposed to and would seriously deter
                    hacking activities and has enacted clear laws
                    against hacking. Rumors about Chinese
                    cyber-espionage are completely unfounded,
                    and those attempting to smear China
                    in this way would not succeed."
Leather jacket   with a seven oz. computer in it,
            from this distance, could be a wind-brought
trashbag in its dark conformity
to the scaffold of branches,
to the *Matthew Passion*
on his headphones, he having stared too long at an ecliptic
                                        band of cloud,
one fork of the now
diffused contrail: wherever he looks,
                        a phosphene effect
                        overlays on the tussocky thatches
                        a wide road of brass, on which he proceeds
to retrieve his jacket, road
that trifurcates his field, the "batteries,"
discharging all   at once, a stream of
ions splitting in his head
the sternly pretty head
of an image of— Abraham? it partheno-
genetically splitting into

Arabic *Ibraahema,*
        an American political cartoon
        of "Judas" (caressing the wing of a bomber) with female hips,
        in a bikini patterned with the flag of France,
and the calm, apolitical face
of Agnosis.

Threshold Clouds

Up a curving road
    on a dry gold hill,
    you follow at thirty paces.

Sometimes I look back and you're there,
    sometimes not.

I came back to northwest California,
    dry grass wind gold ultra blue,
    back to late childhóod, when I lóved yóu.

Shadows of spheroid clouds:
    the hilltop dark
    where the road curves out of sight.

There's a nearly inaudible music,
    sparse, for a single instrument,
    composed posthumously; stopped,
    I stare into the slow collision
    of three clouds.

You stop, out of sight.

Three clouds,
    suddenly familiar, disunite.

How can I know these are not the clouds
    we saw when there was such a thing
    as indestructibility
    ten seconds/years ago, how can I know
    if you're behind me or ahead?

I turn downhill to monitor the clouds
over the coast and sea, not ponderous
intelligences haunted by interstices
of fey blue, not anthropomorphic,
fully alien.

Black Crosses

They climbed a sandstone grade
and rested at the crest to watch

container ships and sundown.
There are too few terms

for gradients of love. They ran
in long coats that turned

to capes. He caught up; she
stopped; he stopped; it is not love,

but lailailai! A whiskey light cross-
cut the strand and the woman

through the man. They stood
spread-armed, footnailed

to their shadows, the black crosses.

Your Brother in the Trees

I walked today in hemlock
woods, following

a creek. Some books
with me, some work

to do. Books you would like,
I think. I found a ruin

of a homestead. The cottage had
a waterwheel, a window broken,

wheel still turning. I began
a longer letter there. Instead,

I sent you this.

I Thought I Saw You Again Today

I thought I saw you again today, a shadow in the dark
blue air behind a tree. I nearly daily run or walk
from the house to within far sight of the sea. Simulacrum
is a place, not you (I left you in my sleep); it's a place
in which absence is sovereign, and sometimes I hear me talk,
stepping past a blue rim of a shadow. I say: *Simulacrum*
is the capital of an ill-defined imperium behind a pine
on a hill in California. I am too protected by this slowness.
In the house and hills and cloud systems. It's in the one
white spot on a tick on a dark brown stone. I run slowly.
Consciousness becomes an exercise. When I write to you,
I am distracted, then made sleepy, by these details, avatars
of slowness: quarter-second graphite scratch, long third
note from a three note bird, Morse code, wind pollen, SOS.

Passat

She read his outdated translation of *Confessions* —
       he had told her it would baffle her
       like altruism baffles those who lack
       a ventromedial cortex.

She left a note on his door: *What could you know*
       about science? Call.

He told her he'd been a boy
       and gone to a hole in a stone wall,
       the end of his mother's land.

Through the hole, it was the same, except
       the neighbor vintner's grapes were small
       and green.

The boy felt nothing could happen.

Insects in the vines made variations
       on the notes he hummed.

A girl's or a delicate boy's hand came through
       the hole and dropped a jade-
       and-red dead dragonfly
       and retracted.

He told her he took the dragonfly
       and, the next day, came amid wind
       and small bees to the hole
       and pushed the book he most loved,
       a sea adventure, through the wall.

The Red Grape

Needing to know about the red light
    in the east vineyard's shed,
    the boy went out there and discovered
    his eldest brother
    holding up a woman's legs
    next to the furnace.

A black dress draped a rack of fire tools.

His naked brother stepped across the woman
    and a rug from Ethiopia
    and pushed the boy from the shed.

Whiffs of bunch rot, boys barefoot in dew—
    or I will break your wrists, the elder said,
    and don't forget that ever, either.

What if I forget?

You won't. Listen,
    her name's Amanda, she drives the car
    you asked about at dinner, parked by the pump—

What?

I said,
    she was a salamander,
    but she asked to have a human body,
    and they get one wish before they die.
    I found her under one red grape
    in a black clump.

No.

No you.

What if I forget?

The larger face half-like the boy's,
        not angry, irrealizing, two half-faces, ten—
        the open hand that'd picked the one red
        clapped against the boy's forehead.

Now you won't forget.
        Bring us some wine from the house?

Lucifer

Behind the house
of the dead naturalist,
I stoop over a fist-sized
amber blob and drive
a stick into it and sniff
the sampling, odorless.
So unfamiliar, this
substance. Maybe bloody
feces of a sudden oak
death dryad. She didn't
suffer much; I heard her;
I was sleeping. Under it,
a carapaced black worm
tightens in the light.
I flip the worm
onto the flipped blob,
and the worm feigns
death. I gently sway,
my shadow aimed east.
A great armored wheel
grinds wood and books
to weird flour in my brain.

Fire Road

Again I hike the fire road.
Forgive my streaked ink,
the sparse
rain is arrowy
and flying

sideways. We left prints
in this — I see
by daylight, not grass,
some kin to mint,
and every other
leaf is red.

I thought you were dying
last night here:
I felt, behind
your breasts,
a clock

eclipsed by a true north compass.
You aren't sick. That was
a counterfeit omen,

something in the coarseness
of your hair as
I cupped

your skull, or that your
skull, that's seen more
ports and highways
than mine, could be
so harrowingly
contained.

Karuk Nation

1

Root, Antler, Fork, Braid

His daughter Root. That wasn't her name,
and he called her that. I found her
at the driveway's end, a cruel-looking girl. I asked
what was she doing out here in the dark.
Come with, if you want.
House built into the hill.
Antlers propped against a propane tank.
He came out with a long, steel, grilling fork
pointed at me, *Your mother's the one*
with ribbons in her braids?

2

CENTER-OF-THE-WORLD

America was not a word here.
Ikxareeyav had been gods. *One god,*
Eel-with-a-Swollen-Belly, lived
at the downstream end of the world
and swam the river-earth and stopped
to stack rocks here on the north side.
Those were singing places for the people.
He stacked rocks on both sides of the river.
He had made the Center-of-the-World.
That's a story for children. It was before dawn.
Huge toppled cairns. *You'll die*
if you fall in, so don't. We crossed
a field of halfsunk stones in the canyon.

3

KARUK PEOPLE

Ninivássi vúra,
vitkiniyâac ta kóova,
tu'áxxaska,
tu'áxxaska—
I slept in the hunting shack
with his mother. He'd planned
to sleep in the tent with mine;
she said *go,* and he stayed out all night
with his gun. Between the boards,
where the shack's mossed wall
had warped, I watched him
run a cloth along his gun
and plug his eye into the scope
aimed into the zodiac.
What kind of cancelled immortality
was this? And yet he was the opposite
of what at twelve I understood
of death. He tilted at the moon.
—*My back,*
it has become like a mountain ridge,
so thin,
so thin.

4

PRAYER FOR ENDING STORIES

He sat in the needles,
thumbing the bone
of his knifehandle.
I stood behind him,
chin on his head.
His mother was
nearly blind.
Her songs were
repetitious and
about extinction.
—*Ninivássi vúra,*
vitkiniyâac ta kóova,
tu'áxxaska,
tu'áxxaska.

Hard Copies

Old man was
dying, out there in

the subsublime,
filmic light,

where hills smoked,
father childer than

the man, the
father's child

who wrote a note,
"Old man was

dying…" on
the back of a receipt

for gasoline. Astronauts
had left this unreal country

to flag
the veridical moon.

Feast of Weeks

Crossroads through redbud
fields of black Ohio,

southwind in my
braid. All references

condensed: a drop
of nectar, dust

and dew: a grain
of rain that flickered: stone

farm fences, thicketry,
a mushroom ring,

a telecom
pylon: a drop

of thought
event horizon.

Second Thaw

Out of witch hazels and pines,
                onto a treeless chine
in the Catskills, not true
orogenic mountains,   a dissected plateau: six flying crows,
and the sequence is
sun cloud
sun:
             in the cold of each cloud,
his mind/body/problem begins to report   his life is departing, barely,
then the signal ceases
as the sun returns: the problem
self-preserves: the people on
computers lost their fear today,
bought back their metal, energy,
technology, and service stocks and currencies and bonds, and he writes
a note to the woman he lives with: *Up here—*
              on my headphones,
              John Tavener's
              Akathist *thanking*
              the Sartre-shaped
              hole in my chest
              full of chambers
              and bells and
              scarlet and blue
              ventricular ferns
              and DNA
              from English, Irish,
              Gypsies, Iroquois,
              and Jews—
              I thank you.
                  Wind turbines on the far ridge turn:
eleven composite-material pegasi,
pulling a planet, yoked amid hundreds
of millions of crude oil
oxen of the sun.

Way to the Wedding

He was looking at a map
       with reverence— place names, traceries,
       the legend— though he did not love
       America, not as it now stood at attention.

In Elyria, Ohio, he telephoned his father.

I've been through Elyria.
       I lost my glasses at a motel there.
       I was eighteen.

I'll look for them.

He stopped at War Axe
       in Nebraska, in the dead bison prairie,
       saw no bones— in No Name, Colorado,
       purchased water in a bottle for $1.98—
       and in Grand Junction, stole the Gideon
       and naked and unshaven read the Song of Songs
       and read it as a red slash in the black
       field of the Tanakh.

Wed, he said to the motel wall.

He felt unsafe and hid the Gideon
       inside a black suit in his bag
       and felt imperfect.

All night he drove to Campo Pesquero La Lobera,
       where Jews stood under palm trees.

Rose of Shar'on. Tents of Kedar.

There was wind—she in her white.

He died at twenty-four and didn't
tell me how.

Better than wine, I will run after you
and catch the foxes in the vineyards
on the day of the wedding,
a strand of scarlet,
henna with spikenard,
and the watchmen struck me,
took my veil away.

We Had a Word for the Two of Us

Campo Pesquero La Lobera, 1939

We didn't read books anymore, just pushed the barrow.

The vegetable plot was weeds.

An orange rope went oak to oak along the cliff.

At dusk, parallel to the sea horizon, the rope became invisible—it had been
 white when we read books.

We'd painted it to match the sun and painted the house, too, orange.

I want you to call me Maria again,
 the child will learn to talk and name us separate sounds.

Certain days the sky was full of little pebble clouds.

We'd been Clement and Maria, then there were too many books about
 wars, so we wrote our names on paper, side by side, and painted white
 over the names and let it dry and wrote one word over that.

I pushed the barrow out toward the sun rope, dropping it halfway, half in
 the weeds— taking the rope in my hands, saying in my head, *child*
 not born, when you walk, never cross here.

I knew Maria spoke rightly— out on the sea, I saw a buoy.

〜

What are you about to do?

I plan to cut the milkweed down.

You can't use that. You have to kill the roots.

White flew from stalks and streaked my clothes.

Maria at the garden's edge, *That's sperm.*

I hacked on and stank in my shirt.

We'll still be us, Maria said. *We aren't Egyptian ancient people.*

Now what do you mean by that?

Nothing you would care.

You had a thought. I'd like to know it.

There she sat on the capsized barrow, face of sloping long lines, hunting looks, brown clothes unmarred by the barrow's rime of dirt, *You love the sun so much… maybe much more than me. Is that a meaningless comparison?*

I said, *Now which Egyptian goddess had the long head of an elegant dog?*

I don't remember if there was a long dog. One had, one head was a cat's.

I'd spoken intimately to the sun since I was four feet high, never looking at the sun directly, contending I could.

I looked at Maria directly, *Maria.*

Swinging the scythe till dusk, till the weed plot stood one inch.

≈

Maria slept—she didn't know where in my head I had already gone, or she did not let on.

I took my jacket from the deer-horn on the wall and walked barelegged and barefoot into the fog, thinking I would cut the sun rope.

I could not—I could not see the sea horizon, one hand on the rope, the other on the scythe, blade down, a crutch.

Away from the cliffs and home, through cold fields, land I knew well, but without the sun, it was not mine.

Beyond a man's length in that fog, no feature, earnest ghost gray all ways.

Scythe across my shoulders, arms draped out as on the shoulders of companions, and the blade curved at the land, then did I look a farmer, angel, crazy man?

And what frayed ropes and parallel horizons mark the no man's lands between the archetypes?

Young once I ran through oak and acres, inland, on the day the sun was not one word.

I knelt in a meadow and knew why my father sat with whiskey by the hearth.

He'd told me flames were Babel tower tongues and spat some whiskey on the embers.

How many trillion tongues then did the sun address, hex, love, bless, and lucify me with the day I knew and knelt and took an orange pebble?

When I threw it straight up at the sun, it did not return.

My father didn't know my face his ending weeks, didn't always know my name— I read to him from books of war, and didn't our obscurer story blur with those of Sherman, Christ, Napoleon, and Moses?

Walking over rock and sage.

I heard moaning.

Wire fence marked my land's edge written in my father's will.

I traced the wire to an unshorn ram, entangled, hindparts bloody, and the
    ram bucked feebly and dirged, too much for wire wounds only, a
    bullet maybe, a coyote.

In my good life, some things came without deliberation—throw a pebble,
    love Maria, orange the house and rope, reap milkweed, manumit
    this ram.

The scythe, inherited with the land, I gripped the shaft and horizontal
    handle, held the tool high at a shaking angle, poised— an iron beak,
    an angel can go crazy—swung.

One foot on the neck, I ripped the tool from a bone.

Thaw pain came with the heat, so I put both feet in the blood.

Then when I'm dead, I want my child to read this.

Child, this is no parable— your father Clement, dead, his feet were cold, he
    loved the sun.

What Are You?

I think of you   at some point in
most hours: maybe standing by   a window
in your birth-black hair   not cut since birth,
never older than eight,   you're still but charged
with weird potential,   posed as if
to have your picture   taken or to be
taken   yourself, away from   me. What are you?
An echo?   *you contain you contain you...*   A child,
an unbreached, little self.   No one   was taken
away from me?

Medal of Honor

Once, in Manhattan, a doctor died
and left a library of poets to her daughter,
who preferred the evening news

and asked me to go, so
I said, the old editions
in green jackets, may I...

In Nebraska City, I live by
silos by the tracks. In Whitman
in his jacket this noon, I came to
a page with edelweiss
pressed on it, and
the petals blocked

a poem, and I said o.
I accept, because
that poem was already
an iron-petaled hieroglyphic
in my brain, and the stem

pointed at another poem: *Here, take this gift,*
I was reserving it for some hero, speaker, or general...

Dying in the Waysong Living

If my inspirants are cracked rocks,
whitewood, water (I pray here,

a rootsman, toeing cracks
the river will arrive in. Rockfish

dry in inch-deep pools
after the sun cracks

the season like red wheat.
Evaporate, freeze.) rhythm locked

to the cosm's clock (Amen
Arcadia and totem omen

hawk), I'm obsolete, circadian.

Troubadour

Often there is a man, who, when he sees
an inch of a woman's back
                exposed
by a shift of her blouse in a public place
                       (a woman
he's never met), no longer
shudders as he once did
                (trumpet
full of blood) for conquest
and/or chivalry. Instead,
              he *knows*
he knows the triumphant, full arc of her back.
                      His brain
has been pattern-trained
so completely in courtship, unveiling,
carnality, loss, it's condensed
the pattern
to two steps, first sight,
              then old wistfulness,
and he's not yet old.

Curing Death

The halls of
art and science.
Hot autumn.
She wants to
sleep in grass
and feed
upon apples
and strawberries.
My beard
hairs lengthen
imperceptibly.
Her clothes were
sewn in Italy.

Life on Europa

imagine you
with a talent for thinking (suspending)
at once many layers and axes of
        asymmetry
and symmetry,
        across which synaptic traffic is
interlaced sense and non sequitur: magnetic
               North Pole:
come down, sorrow
cosmonauts, pimps, with your barber-pole lances and copies of *Ivanhoe*:
under the catwalk,
the polished stage of cloud-colored wood,
backdropped by a silkscreen of
Yggdrasil with branches bearing:
               runes, nests, hailstones, small
               nations, gnawed
               dragonfruit, fierce multinational
food corporations, and anything else you think up
before my guess at what
your mind suspends breaks up   like debris
               from orbit, falling

into the ionosphere,   and is occluded
by the cloud at the fringe of the Tree of Moves   in a mind with a talent for chess.

imagine you sheathing your weapons,
removing your crown and capuchin:
you're a well-paid soprano, Wagnerian,
come now from world-touring, tired, eating toast
with cloudberry jam and poached eggs:
        you have no time tonight for axes,
        your mother has uterine cancer:
        I would like to be alone,

so: the whiteness of
the discarded shells
is the whiteness of calcium carbonate

                                        of which they're made,
                                        though not all eggs
                                        are white. The eggs of passerines,
wherever calcium is thin,
get pigmented with protoporphyrins,
red-browns like the rooftops of Florence observed
from the top of the Duomo, from which many Shintos, Hindus, Jews
take pictures of the final moments of the Renaissance,
through the grid of wire
that keeps their children from tumbling down
                                        the elegant
                                        slope of the dome
                                        into the death of the Renaissance
                                        at the fringe of the tree.

I Come to Bury Caesar

The train
stops in
a region
of fields.

Italians say
there's a cow
on the tracks.

What are you
writing in your teacup
with a pointed sugar-
breaking spoon?

Shadows of Morse
clouds crossing
the fields.

At a Chapel of the Jesuits

Today I'm a Jew. Saints' likenesses man
                            the buttresses.
I keep saying
            peace to myself since I've been in Italy,
I don't know why,
                breaking the word
into homonyms
                and little dead coals. I do wish
I knew what this is, what promise more
alluring than standard heaven—or
is heavensoon the only thought
that makes an old man on his knees
beside me rock and hold his smiling head? A choir
from speakers hidden in the saints. Arrows, light
from candles and arrowslit windows. Bells, but
not from this chapel. A clock on the wall
and a watch on my wrist. The latter breaks
                            a shaft
into prismatics and my eye, the one punched last night.

Tahnee

Tahnee's alone
in the palazzo

courtyard, at the bar
beneath the luna

marble overhang
that shields the cups

and beans and bottles
of cream from rain

and falling petals
from the bougainvillea

on the windowbars and walls.

Beautiful without Money

Suddenly fatigued among French
women in the Roman

Empire rooms of the museum,
I fall out of circulation

on a bench. Bronze
heads, helms, a Byzantine

spoon, 6th century, engraved,
attributed to Virgil: *O handsome*

youth, do not believe
too much in beauty; you cannot be

beautiful without money… women fall,
tucking skirts, onto my bench,

being suddenly flesh and scent,
and do not speak to me.

Open Window

Sometimes when you sing at night, a dried rose brown
obscurity unfolds and folds behind my eyes.
I'm in a sad, small, merciful place.
One could call me a fraction
of a narrow persona, a secondary character
in a tale no longer told to children.
No one knows why he goes or comes.
Sometimes he asks you to sing. He alone asks you that;
he's at peace in a way few would want to be.
This mood: under the whirling oars
of a ceiling fan somewhere in Europe, a continent
with roots (exposed
above the ground as alps and neoclassical hotels
and obelisks stolen from Egypt) soft enough to sleep on.

In Goriška
For L.

The train slows,
    speeds, and you come back,
    not talking, settling across from me, solving the
little riddle of living in the middle of eternity untroubled by the rhythm of the ties
    which is, for me, a measuring of time,
    foreshortening to a false depth
    my sense of age,
    of having traveled,
    but I think to you
an instant is no more a point of departure than an unasked question— I said
    last night, "What time is it?"
    I said it again. "I thought
    you hadn't asked," you said.

Flicker

For T.

You hold a teacup—don't be unsteady.
You might ruin the hardwood.
You say you like the raw world
but don't travel.

Past the border of the city,
perched in a tree's crotch,
I flick gnats with a whippy stick.

I have no trade, no
tea. I wish you would find
a train, the one no one rides,
and a fire-colored dress, so

I can find you in the blue
and say we petrify like gods—
a classicist unearths our kissing heads.

Behind the Prytaneum

Tragedy began with a dance in the guise of goats, said Aristotle.
Tragedy began with a sacrifice of goats, said Eratosthenes.
They came to a circle of columns or great white trees.
They drank red resveratrol wine from the bottle.
A classicist shouts, *those are not differing accounts!*
One must kill a goat to dress as a satyr.
Way of necessity, way of the wine, a fluid ounce —
in Galilee, where he has turned, said John, *the water into rhyme,*
a god's son or a vintner dies, not differing accounts
when laser diode udometers measure, millennia later,
the rainfall on fields that yield grapes for wine —
a miracle's a narrative with time
condensed. *An ounce for the gorgeous man in the gutter,*
the beggar-poet cries, *and some crab legs with clarified butter!*

House with a Dark Sky Roof

My brother's Greek wife told him, if he loved her, he would live on her untouristed
island, where a meditative life is hard to tell apart from stasis:

                                                                    I aged,
and he didn't. He wrote and called,

and his voice was sad
and young without virility.

                    He walked,

looking down at the violets and lovage,
plants typically strewn

at the feet of the dead, or, if he raised
his head, alders, cypresses,

                              black poplars, trees
of the dead, and he called and said: *She's athletic, wiser, readier than I. The sex sometimes
defeats me. She turns off the lights too early at night. She makes me forget things. Her dog is
mean. Anyone who comes into this house, she marks his height on the doorpost.*

10,000th Bad Ithaca Dream

Zeroes file out of the stock market
into the ranks of punk, cigarette-
spitting priests of the streets. *Temenos
breached!* Furies in menopause
pick through a tin of nitrated livers.
Dead end of an elongated universe:
light and iron, little else, no radio
signals from earlier Ithacas. *Dios mio,*
says a Fury in an orchid porkpie hat.
Short sold my children, says a zero, at
the corner of Broadway and Via
Del Corso. Kings sink in absentia,
but one severe, backlit Penelope's
out on a pier with an open envelope.

Islands

She left him on Ithaca, Cuba, Manhattan.
He studied telomere strands.
  An ankh-symbol traced on her back with his hand—

the man in a long white coat, who knelt at the end of the pier.
He studied shortening telomere strands.
  He read a dead letter, found in his hand.

Kurofune, black ships, burned coal, from the West
to Japan. She left him in line
at the symphony, and (it was Mendelssohn's
Hebrides, so he was crying) the rest
of a decade he studied the strands.
  He read a map of her x-rayed hand.

Drakkar, caravel, black ironclad—
"Come back, Miranda," he wrote to her and—
destroyer, biplane, Apollo 11, then
what shape's the next ship we build if we can?
Halfway to the end of the pier (half of half, then
  half of that), strands of her letters.

Quintet at Café Objet du Ciel Profond
Geneva, 2009

To start at the omega point, that is, to feed
      the first notes of the melody
inverted back into the open
            spaces in the
cymbal ride
pattern backbone in this five
           bar form:
drums
                alto
         bass
                  piano
      horn:
the introduction ends: the melody
          reverts to uninverted Davis
             so
    what
             so
    what: if classical origins, Debussy
                maybe, recessive Schumann:
                into a quiet icefield with
         jagged xenoliths,
      fragments of tugboats,
and derelict lighthouses.   Endnotes
to the books of de Chardin   drift in wind
          with origins
in Africa
from dune   to snowy dune,
            so
    what   notes laced with
fingerprints laced
with DNA   with origins
in Africa:
restatement of the   melody's clipped
                  wings and
      beakholes   in brass

melting back to the copper of wires on the floor
        and the zinc of the bar: zinc, jammed
        with an alpha
        particle,   becomes
           germanium
to build the chip
        that governs the echo effect
        in the pedal-box
        the bassist kicks
to start back toward omega:
     horn   and alto imitate
     the gauntlet of speech
     rhythms,   not only Swiss and French French but:
     French-accented, poolhall, Liberian,
     New York,   New Orleans, Shakespearean
     Englishes, last of which
leads to the   alto solo,
drums back to pentameter, the melody abandoned
        on a rogue moon
        spinning on the mixing board
        back by the WC,
        a solo so
        décousu, so
        abstruse it is
        as if someone has left,
        in a torn suede jacket left
        on a chair at the bar, this note:
        To Whom it May Concern, I was unsound.
        I brindled my black limbs, and since I was
        a virgin, staggered from the hippodrome.
        The rich are tired of the toothless: true.
        A girl, my clone, hawks wheat-corn to the men
        who do abortions for a ha-penny.
        What length's the implement? It pricks a third
        eye on my baby in me. This one has

prepared my flesh with shallow cuts and urns
of water marathons. The sacrifice:
I will be bound up, ankles, wrists, and thighs.
My clone will hawk the heartmeat for a ha.
I found a penknife in the parking lot,
blade from a bar of Bonivard's portcullis,
stock of brass and horse-horn, circlet from
a sundog's bone. I thought this Pen would rip
new noise, new as a jazz quintet upon
the stunnéd fops and maniacs, the year
1616, House of Savoy. I drove
like hellebores out on the Voie Centrale,
good brut, and skidding on the shoulder, deep
in herbage, blasting out the moonroof, through
the canopy into the sheaves of blue
to write on the horizon: "Once I spake
in Saxon circles. Du, mein kleine Klon,
do not give birth to you. You pay the men."
A luciferin marrow spilt from stalks
to freeze in dun drops onto dead sun leaves.
I ruptured from the wood at cocaine speed
and wrecked on parkbenches in Chambery.
The horn takes off the gauntlet and demands
"satisfaction!" throwing it down:
> piano hinting at a third
> hand, invisible, right of the right hand,
> off the sonic
> keyboard, teleonomizing cloud
formations into animal
approximations, riots
into national self-criticism,
wings (evolving separately
on birds, bats, pterosaurs
and insects) into angel-given
> missions to an insubstantial world.

Repeating

                        structures

            and

                         the chord

        progression:

replicating

                        structures

           saturate

                        the universe

        with Mind?

The special ending variation's like

a sermon by a freak Don Juan,

              who puts the jacket on

          and leaves the bar

                  and tells her in the car:

    I'll dragonfly my tongue

          on your flawstruck pearl.

    Haneek rabbak,

          the night advances.

   Is there not an evidence

         in two young ancients

   in a platinum car

         that's a blood-thinning pill,

   for an impotent

        God! I'm yelling louder than the radio,

             This force we found tonight, gesticulating

               one hand off the wheel, *it's nearly nothing*

      as the destinations simplify and halve

and halve becoming

all is one!   the speed the coming

God, *We must be*

      more than nothing

but a love song stuck

     between notes.

Promethean Factors Engineering

Noel Byron didn't think
angels existed outside ink and died of leeches.
He begged "his British godship's humble pardon
if in my extremity of rhyme's distress
I touch a single leaf where he is warden; —" Byron had
bad bones exacerbated by bad
braces, so he hurt to stand in his abridged life.

Happy is England? and the rest
of the First World nobility when, in this
intelligent chapter, bolts strike
with no god's warrant, and titanium knits
a better foot than bone.

At Keats Grove, Hampstead

A blaze beneath a blossom
tree, a wind forks

wind and names—hail
fire, green John—saint me.

Whose nest fits on a grassblade?
But I have to go now.

Writ in blank rest, please—
this house, I—

stedfast as thou
blazing shade—

I wish to not die.

Broken Stair

For G. K.

1

I ride your motorcycle into town
and buy pork and tortillas.

Back at Broken Stair,
I eat
with two stub candles for light
and sit

a long time, until the sun
and another from years ago come up
with interlocking haloes,

and the twice-bright zone
occults a star
Old English called Éarendel.

2

My glasses
put the suns into each other.
I drink water
with a cupric taste

from the spigot.
In the floor-stones,
I can feel

machinery a mile off building
a road out of this country.

Haku

Forktailed star-hooded
diving birds: in Hawai'i,
haku is crown of

flowers: *haku* of
haiku: my sunflower of
shadows turning on

birds of stark old age,
paradise pinions bone gray:
light-years of youth crowned

the clockless wall: blown
fey petals, my flashforward
minutes of old age.

Calls

Night dogs in the city
sound their skulls

like conch horns. We
forget each other's words

from phone to satellite to phone
calls last year. By now, maybe

voices in the Oort
Cloud, light-seconds apart,

keep on in conversation
if an Oortshell sounds them back

like Earthshells do the ocean.

The Wild Clarifying

Have you been anywhere?
Manhattan, Italy, Slovenia

and Mexico, I was
in Galilee and California.

Territories, dead coins,
avarice and beauty alloyed,

and a vulpine grace:
all this in her blackly

made-up face, beauty
like fields of blood only

if "fields of blood"
in a poem's black ink. It comes,

the wild clarifying
flash rain over fields. Mint

Rome and Nahariya on her eyelids
shut. She says she thinks she tried

suicide last year:
to go somewhere.

Elsewhere

Nine years since I've seen you,
and you dislike telephones.

And you won't write back.
I want to tell you what I did today.

Only to think of you thinking it—
and I will leave out anything banal

in periphery I might have passed—
only to relate a safe piece of my day on Earth,

and maybe you can see
me in your head,

if that's where you are.

John Golden's Sign

A fallen V-shaped branch,
                hooked on a lower straight branch
tells with its rocking
the wind's direction,
rocking on the axle of the low branch
in the vertex
of the V. He goes
the opposite direction of the wind,
off the trail, into a rising   clearing with a far
hills panorama at the vertex of the light
land-in-eye and land in   flown-open mind:
a forward-flowing
sky subtracted from an equal backward: just this,
zero, origin:
just what he strictly sees minus anything
"seen" yet imagined, willed,
like here at the edge of thick woods at the edge of the clearing,
a faded square of metal-brown
material: daguerreotype
of Darwin in an earthquaked, leaning tree:

> *If you could feel how exposed we are*
> *to every wind under Heaven,*
> *you would understand our strong wish*
> *to have one sheltered walk,*

then voice and effigy
vague-out like thoughts on outer branches of a mind
that wonders if there's more than metaphorical connection
between *thinking*
thought of
as a tree
and dendrites' physicality:
        metaphors of thought-as-tree
are numerous in history
before the branching
structure at the microscale was known,

and what he'd "seen"
as Darwin, nailed to the deadwood,
strictly is: POSTED
PRIVATE PROPERTY
HUNTING FISHING TRAPPING OR
TRESPASSING FOR ANY PURPOSE
IS STRICTLY FORBIDDEN
VIOLATORS WILL BE PROSECUTED
OWNER: "John Golden"
ADDRESS: here the sign is
rusted away,
and he enters the woods,
being without any purpose.

Notes

"Threshold Clouds"
   Hart Crane wrote to Waldo Frank that "there is such a thing
   as indestructibility."

"Black Crosses"
   These are the lai-lai-lais of praise and chorus
   in traditional Ladino, Arabic, and Hebrew songs.

"Medal of Honor"
   The quote is from "To a Certain Cantatrice."

"Promethean Factors Engineering"
   The quote is from *Don Juan,* Canto Fourteenth, 75th stanza.

"John Golden's Sign"
   The italics are from Darwin's letter to John Lubbock, Jan 16,
   1846.

Lightning Source UK Ltd.
Milton Keynes UK
UKOW050440170911

178816UK00001B/38/P